JEWISH IDENTITY GAMES

A HOW-TO-DO-IT BOOK

RICHARD J. ISRAEL

TORAH AURA PRODUCTIONS

TO SHERRY

MY WIFE AND CO-WORKER IN THE ENTERPRISE OF JEWISH
IDENTITY.

Copyright © 1978 Richard J. Israel

First edition published by B'nai B'rith Hillel Foundations

Second edition, 1993

Second edition published by Torah Aura Productions

Library of Congress Cataloging-in-Publication Data

Israel, Richard J.
Jewish identity games : a how-to-do-it book / Richard J. Israel. --2nd ed.
p. cm.
Includes bibliographical references.
ISBN 0-933873-77-8 : $12.95
1. Games in Jewish religious education. 2. Jews--Identity.
I. Title.
BM125.I84 1993
296.6'8--dc20
93-7896
CIP

Torah Aura Productions
4423 Fruitland Avenue
Los Angeles, California 90058

MANUFACTURED IN THE UNITED STATES OF AMERICA

TABLE OF CONTENTS

PREFACE

This text originally emerged from workshops I conducted for B'nai B'rith Hillel Foundation personnel in Montreal, Boston, Cleveland, and at the Hillel Directors Conference. That is why many exercises presume situations and settings that would commonly be encountered when working with college students. Others were developed at UAHC and Ramah Camps. The family education exercises were used in workshops conducted at Temple Emunah of Lexington, Massachusetts.

The book is directed to people with better-than-average Jewish educations and experience in group work but does not assume any additional specialized skills.

Those who are not at home with the jargon and tools of the Jewish educator may find some of the references a bit cryptic, but probably not so difficult that they would be unusable. I have intended these exercises to be accessible to those who work on campus, in Jewish schools, and with Jewish family life education groups, as well as by human relations professionals who only occasionally work in Jewish settings.

Although this text is copyrighted, there are few implied restrictions concerning the reproduction of its contents. The exercises have been arranged so that users can copy individual exercises easily. They should feel free to duplicate or modify them. Please do not copy the entire book or publish exercises here in other collections without permission.

Suggestions by readers for additional exercises would be welcomed and fully acknowledged in any future edition.

I am available to conduct workshops demonstrating the uses of these exercises.

I wish to express my appreciation to Bernard Reisman, not only for specific exercises to which he and his students introduced me, but also for helping me to think about the field in a new way. Special thanks are due to Samuel Z. Fishman for his friendship, for encouraging me to commit these materials to writing, for his felicitous editing, and for seeing it through to its original publication.

Richard J. Israel
Newton Centre, Massachusetts

INTRODUCTION

The *Jewish Identity Game* is a Jewish adaptation of a methodology that originates in the encounter and values clarification movements. In a way, it is a response to the question that was put so often to Jewish professionals who came early to human relation training groups (often called T-Groups) and group dynamics: "What's Jewish about all this?" Sometimes the practitioners responded by suggesting that if it were important humanly, that was Jewish enough, but when we talked to one another we found ourselves asking the same question.

The question was answered partially after the publication of *Reform is a Verb* (Fein, et al., UAHC, 1972), which had a supplement for professionals that contained a series of "Jewish" exercises designed to enhance the quality of life of the Reform synagogue. Since that time, Jewish "games" have been used widely in Reform synagogues and camps and among federation leadership. There are even circles where their announcement will produce groans: "Oh, not that again!" In some places they are avant-garde, in others old hat, but in any case, they are probably here to stay.

The term *Jewish Identity Games* is short for a group of exercises designed to encourage people to think and talk about Jewish issues in public situations. They are a relatively neutral tool that can be used to enhance conceptual learning, develop a supportive emotional climate in a group, or help people discuss hard but important issues. Games like these can be used to focus a group on specific Jewish interests, such as male and female in the Jewish community, readying oneself spiritually for the Days of Awe, improving the organization of a youth group or a Hillel Foundation, the value of prayer, tzedakah, remembering the Holocaust, etc. They can be used by themselves as effective programs or as a "quick fix" in an emergency, but they are most helpful when they function in a larger framework such as a class or a *Shabbaton*. The usual pattern that these exercises follow is to experience, describe, generalize (if justified), process, and evaluate.

There are any number of texts coming from the human potential movement that include variants of these games without specific Jewish referents. Some of the texts are mentioned at the end of this book. In fact, some of the games included here may already have been so adapted; in many cases I am no longer certain. Where possible, my sources for exercises are identified. I have not tried to identify their originators; that is an unmanageable task. I have tried to give credit to the people from whom I have learned them. If no source is noted, that is because I believe (I hope with justification) that I "invented" the game, or because I no longer have the vaguest idea where I learned it, or because it is so much a part of the shared language of the "trade" that no one can claim to have "invented" it.

The reader who has not used games like these previously is advised to read carefully *Double Circles*, p. 15, *Hillel Says*, p. 29, *Reviewing an Exercise and Moving On*, p. 34, *Further Cautionary Notes*, p. 90, and *A Worry List*, p. 93 , before proceeding to try any of them. These sections provide general guidance. The rest of the exercises more or less stand on their own and do not require a familiarity with all of the others. The exercises that come later in the book are described in less detail than the early ones, on the assumption that the reader has already become familiar with the methodology.

DEMOGRAPHY OF THE GROUP

This is a good warm-up exercise for many group situations. I often use it before I give a talk or start a workshop. It both engages the participants and gives the leader a better sense of who is present. The questions should be adjusted to the nature of the gathering and to what will follow.

This is one way to open:

> "Before we start, first we should do some demography, some head counting to find out who is here. Many of you may know these things already, but let us all get a chance to see who is here by how you answer some questions."

JEWISH EDUCATIONAL BACKGROUND

Have college-level Jewish training?

High school-level Jewish education?

Elementary school?

No formal Jewish schooling at all?

MOBILITY

Were born within one hundred miles of here? In the Northeast? Midwest? South? West? Canada, in Europe, Africa? in the Mideast? Elsewhere?

Were parents born here? Grandparents? etc.

(Is this a local group or essentially outsiders to where they are now living?)

RELATIONSHIP TO FAMILY AND ITS VALUES

Have children?

Have teenage children?

Have siblings? Younger? Older? How many?

How many siblings do your parents have? Grandparents?

Have living grandparents?

Consider yourselves religious Jews? Observant Jews?

Consider yourselves Conservative Jews? Orthodox? Reform? Reconstructionist? Secular? Zionist? other?

JEWISH BEHAVIOR

Have you visited Israel? 1X? 2X? 3X?

Subscribe to a Jewish magazine that is not sent to you because you are a member of an organization?

Speak or understand: Hebrew, Yiddish, Ladino, other non-English language?

Have a *mezuzah* on your door?

Have kosher homes? Eat kosher out?

Keep pork and shellfish out of your homes?

Refrain from eating pork and shellfish out of your home?

Went to a seder last year? (Everyone?)

Lit <u>H</u>anukkah candles this year or present when someone else did?

Were in the synagogue for the High Holidays? For Shabbat last week? (But not to attend a *Bar* or *Bat Mitzvah*)

JEWISH ASSOCIATIONAL PATTERNS

Have mostly Jewish friends?

Would mind if your children intermarried? If they became Christians?

Are you more Jewish than your parents? Less?

WINDUP

Any observations about what we have learned? Are we who you would have expected? Any surprises?

PERSONAL AND JEWISH EXPLORATIONS

DOUBLE CIRCLES

Double Circles is a basic exercise. If the content is varied, it can be used for many purposes, usually as a first exercise (or after "Demography").

Two circles of people (preferably in chairs) sit facing one another, outside circle facing in, inside circle facing out. Each person faces a partner from the opposite circle. If people don't know each other, they should first introduce themselves to their partners in the opposite circle.

Most of the questions discussed throughout this exercise should relate to your specific goals for the participants. Your first question, however, is a throwaway. The participants are just warming up and rarely take it seriously. My favorite first questions are:

How did you happen to come to this gathering? or:

What are your goals and expectations for this weekend (meeting, Shabbaton, etc.)?

Sometimes I prefer "How do you feel right now?" When I use it as the first question I often like to use it as the last question as well. This helps the members to gain some perspective on how much the climate of the group has changed since it began.

Questions are discussed only between the partners, not out in the open. At the end of each question one of the circles shifts and moves one place (always in the same direction), so that people shift their way around the room question by question. They are thus afforded the opportunity to share some relatively intimate thoughts in a large group. Since they interact with only one person at a time, even shy people will usually speak easily; because they speak with many people, a sense of sharing within a community is experienced at the same time.

Another vir.tue of this exercise is that, because the partnerships keep changing, people don't need to panic at the possibility of being stuck with a single person for the entire session or to be particularly troubled if the sex ratio of the group is askew.

After the initial warm-up question, some of the following questions might be asked. It is not an exhaustive list. New questions can be devised to suit the occasion. Some question clusters are too similar to one another to be used at a single session.

SAMPLE QUESTIONS AND THEIR CONTEXTS

JEWISH RELIGIOUS LIFE

What mitzvot are important to your personality?

What Jewish ideas are important to you?

Can you talk about someone who has been a positive or negative religious model for your life?

Do you want to become more Jewish? If so, what is keeping you from it?

REFLECTIONS ON BEING A STUDENT

What was a high point of your last year?

What do you plan to be doing five years from now?

What did you really learn in school this year?

From whom did you learn it? Is that person significant in your life?

Is school a waste of time?

PERSONAL JEWISH SITUATION

What was a Jewish "high" for you this year? A Jewish "low"?

What makes you feel good about being Jewish? What bad?

Who is a Jew you really love? Really hate?

What was a good or bad thing in your Jewish education?

What good thing happened to you this year because you were Jewish? What bad thing?

Is there anything Jewish that embarrasses you?

Do you care whether your friends are Jewish?

Do you care if Israel is in trouble?

Do you care whether you intermarry?

Do you care if your children become Presbyterians?

Do you care if your children join a cult?

Pre–Yom Kippur Workshop

What really makes you happy?

What are you very good at? (Brag!)

What do you really regret doing or not doing last year?

Whom did you wish you hadn't hurt?

Who has disappointed you recently?

How would you want to do things differently in the coming year?

What opportunity did you waste last year?

Are there any goals you would like to set for yourself for next year?

Post-Vacation Workshop

Students have mixed feelings about being at home. These feelings are worth sharing so that individuals may learn that they are not alone. This same exercise can be used with minor changes in wording if they went on vacation with their families rather than remaining at home.

What was good about being at home?

What was bad about being home?

What is good about being back in school? What is bad?

Who were the people you were happy to see when you got back to school?

Who were the people you were happy to see when you were at home?

Describe one of your parents.

If you were one of your parents, how would that parent describe you?

Parent-Child Interchange (In Double Circles)

This exercise can be used for some very good parent-child conversations. What makes it work is that the questions dissolve the generation gap by making the parents remember what it was like to be a child.

What is good thing your parents did for you?

What is a rotten thing your parents did to you?

What is a good thing you did for your parents?

What is a rotten thing you did to your parents?

After a warm-up using these four questions in Double Circles you have a lot for parents and children to talk about together. In this exercise it is very important to have general talk afterwards. This will encourage parents and children to talk with one another about the issues they have just discussed with other people's parents and children. The following exercises are variations on this one.

Parent-Child Workshop for 5th and 6th Grades

Warm-up: Raise hands to answer and discuss in total group:

1. How many of you were born in the same city your parent/s were?
2. How many of you have more brothers and sisters than your parent/s? Fewer than? Same number?
3. Is it easier to be a parent or a child? Who here thinks it is easier to be: A child? The parent of a child?
4. What is easier about it?
5. Who here thinks it would have been best to be a: First child? Middle child? Last child? Only child? Makes no difference?
6. How many of you are/were in the family position you thought would have been best? How many are not?
7. How many of you can do something your parent/s can't or couldn't do? Tell us some of these things.

Then move into Double Circles (each Double Circle will consist of one circle of parents and another of children. Try not to pair up children with their own parents within the Double Circle.)

1. Introduce yourself.
2. Have you had a teacher you really liked? Couldn't stand?

3. Talk about a nice thing your parents did for you that made you feel terrific.

4. Talk about a rotten thing your parent/s did to you that made you really angry.

5. Talk about a nice thing you did for your parents that made them feel terrific.

6. Talk about a rotten thing you did that made your parents really angry.

To the total group:

> Any questions that were particularly easy or hard to talk about?
> Anything else to report from the discussion?

Finally, brainstorm in two separate groups—one for parents, one for kids—in one large room and make a list (one staff facilitator in each group—see "Warring Camps" page 56).

1. Parent/s—what is wrong with your kids?

2. Kids—what is wrong with your parent/s?

3. Swap lists, then discuss: "What might you have done that made them say those things about you?"

Reassemble and alllow time for whole group to talk about what has been learned.

PARENT-CHILD WORKSHOP FOR 3RD TO 8TH GRADE

In Double Circles, with a circle of children facing a circle of parents, try tgo keep children out of conversational contacts with their own parents. Frst introduce yourself, then:

1. The Jewish holiday I like best is…and the one
   I like least is…

2. If I could tell God what to do, this is what I would say:

3. Something I thought was really funny was…

4. Something I thought was really funny, but my parents didn't think was funny at all, was…

5. A scary experience I once had was…

6. Once when I had a really good time with my parent/s…

7. What really made my parents mad was when I…

8. It really made me mad when my parents…

9. A time I lied and got caught was…

10. A time I lied and didn't get caught was…

Reassemble:

What have you learned?

Then, in separate groups: (5th to 8th grades—not younger)

Parents: If your child said:

Children: If you said:

"I think we should have a Christmas tree, just like the rest of my friends," a good parent would say…

"My friend and I were playing in the living room, and we just broke the big double glass window," a good parent would say…

"I can't stand going to Junior Congregation," a good parent would say…

"One of the kids at school said he didn't want to play with me because I am Jewish," a good parent would say…

"There is something important going on at public school on the day of Yom Kippur, and I want to go," a good parent would say…

How close should we expect a good parent/child to be to a real one?

Let's all gather together and talk about our answers.

Some Miscellaneous Questions for Double Circles

What is the one thing that others can do for you that will make you happy? (After the men get over their initial guffaws, they will generally get down to business.)

Talk about a situation in which you were embarrassed.

What is a personal achievement of which you are proud?

When were you lonely this year, and why?

In your next incarnation, what kind of person would you want to be?

Tell about your name—what it means to you, what associations you have with it, how it fits into the rest of your life and your family, and what it may mean to this group.

After the flood, which agencies of the Jewish community would you rebuild in what order?

One thing I don't understand about Jews is…

Why do some Jews…

TEACHING RESPONSA IN DOUBLE CIRCLES

(FROM JERROLD GOLDSTEIN)

After the subject has been introduced and the partners have met each other, present each person in the group with a responsum, a classic Jewish legal question. One source of responsa is *A Treasury of Responsa*, by Solomon B. Freehof (J.P.S., Philadelphia, 1963). A more recent collection of questions is found in *Current Halachic Problems*, by J. David Bleich (Ktav, N.Y., 1977). Reform responsa are found in the Freehof volumes: *Reform Responsa, Current Reform Responsa, Recent Reform Responsa*, etc. (H.U.C. Press, Cincinnati). After the pairs have had five minutes to discuss a question, present them with the written text of the responsum. If the material is complex, let the partners teach it to each other.

When the circles have moved through three or four questions, have a general discussion with the entire group.

GENERAL SUGGESTIONS FOR DOUBLE CIRCLES

When constructing questions, don't get into very personal issues until you sense that the group feels comfortable discussing them. If a question doesn't go well, move on to the next one.

It is important that the number of people in the inside and outside circles be equal. When you have an uneven number in one of the circles you might want to use an extra staff person who can be drawn out of the exercise later if an additional participant arrives.

Things go best if each participant has at least one discussion with each of the people in the opposite circle. Assuming six or eight questions (more than ten would be boring), your ideal number of people would be twelve to sixteen; however, one question for each pair in the circle is not essential. The exercise can be done with a minimum of four people per circle (eight participants) or a maximum of fifteen (thirty participants).

I have worked comfortably with up to thirty people by myself (two circles of fifteen each), but when the group gets larger than that I prefer to work with several sets of circles simultaneously. Then an assistant and I wander about helping people to focus on the project, particularly at the beginning before they have settled into the exercise. If people are giggling in a corner, the staff person might walk over and ask: "Are there any problems here? Do you need any help? Do you understand the instructions? If you don't feel comfortable participating, could you try to hold down the noise?" The tone of the questions should be neither tentative nor dictatorial. If one group doesn't want to participate, it shouldn't have to. On the other hand, it shouldn't have the right to disturb the others.

Good friends or intimates should be discouraged from sitting next to each other. It is hard to concentrate on your discussion partner if a real-life partner is saying some important things right next to you. Real-life partners should be encouraged to sit a few seats apart in the same circle so that they do not distract each other. They have enough time for private conversation elsewhere. You may have a problem when people who haven't been in touch for years discover each other or become excited when they find that they have had friends in common. In most instances the problem is solved after the first shift, and they reconcile themselves to continuing the conversation at the end of the exercise.

Each question should take about five minutes. You may want to make that time longer or shorter, depending upon the subject matter or mood of the group. The participants need to know how many minutes they will be permitted to talk and how much time remains. They should be told explicitly to allow enough time for each of the partners to speak. You should note the time which you ask the question, for it is difficult to maintain a sense of how long each discussion has been going on. In these situations time has a way of becoming very elastic. The same number of minutes will sometimes seem long, sometimes brief to the person directing the exercise.

People will begin to feel manipulated relatively quickly, particularly if the discussion is successful. They won't want to keep moving around the circle but will want to continue talking where they are. You should warn them in advance that this may happen.

The questions are raised orally by the leader. The best way to introduce them is at the end of each discussion and before one of the circles has shifted:

"The issue to be discussed after the next move is _____.
Please shift and introduce yourself to your next partner."

It is hard to break off the discussion if you ask them to move before announcing the next question.

It is important to plan the sequence of your questions in advance. Don't just improvise. You may choose to "over-plan," anticipating that you will skip some questions on your list, but you should know beforehand what your potential questions are going to be. This is the only way you can be sure that they will build upon one another in appropriate order. If you are interested in having people discuss the problems of being Jewish, your questions should move toward that subject. If you want to have a social evening, the questions should lead to the social activities that will follow. If you want to conclude with study of a Jewish text, the questions should gradually bring you to that point.

Try not to ask about superlatives: the best, the worst, the most anything. If you do that, people may clutch and not be able to talk at all. On the other hand, if you ask them to discuss not their best experience or lowest point in the year, but rather a good experience or a low point, they will almost always talk about their best experiences and lowest points.

When you have finished the questioning, ask the groups to stop. Then, in general forum, ask: "What happened? How did it go?" It should be very clear (without your stating so explicitly) that there are no right or wrong answers to a question. Your role is to be a facilitator and to validate all kinds of things that people say. You should not allow debates that suggest that this group of people talked about the right things and that one the wrong things. Ask if people found it hard to get into the exercise, so that if there are some who reacted negatively, they, too, will have a chance to say so. In all of this you are modeling the sort of behavior you want everyone in the group to manifest: You are trying to create a non-judgmental atmosphere in which people will find it easy to talk about important subjects.

You will usually want to use Double Circles in combination with other exercises. For example, if you wish to promote serious Jewish reflection, ask a series of "Jewish values" questions in Double Circles. Then use the Hillel Says exercise that follows. When it is finished you can be prepared with a snappy Jewish credo of your own. Deliver it and let the participants respond. Or have the group study someone else's written credo in pairs, one-on-one Bet Midrash Hevruta style, teaching and reading to each other. Then have a general discussion.

You can use variations of Double Circles again as long as you don't drag it out too long. It can be used more than once with the same group. The exercise can be kept fresh because it is so straightforward and non-gimmicky. Be wary, though. If they begin to tire of it, drop it in favor of other techniques.

HILLEL SAYS

Take your Double Circles apart and form single circles of no more than five or six people. Have everyone sit down. Ask each small circle to have one person at a time stand up and answer one of the following questions that you have selected:

> What is really important to you?
>
> What is the essence of your Jewishness?
>
> The most important thing about being Jewish for me is …

But they can only talk for as long as they are standing on one foot. People can say very important things in that period of time, but they cannot exhaust or harangue the group with excessive chatter. Though people tend to take the assignment seriously, they cannot be overly earnest while teetering on one leg. That is all to the good.

One way of using Hillel Says is to start by asking the participants to discuss "What is really important to you," and then to follow up with a second question (you judge whether it should be standing or sitting): "What is the most important **Jewish** thing to you?" Then ask the participants to discuss the discrepancy between the two responses. It may be startling for people who think of themselves as committed Jews to discover the extent to which what matters most to them has little to do with their being Jewish.

You may want to conclude with participants sharing brief Jewish autobiographies in their small groups. (A very good exercise for adults.)

PEOPLE-GRAMS

In this exercise participants are asked to take a position (literally!) on a series of Jewish issues as a basis for the discussion to follow. The exercise is suitable for eight to twenty people. Its format allows for an infinite number of variations. The examples are given by way of illustration. The instructions might go as follows:

> How religious do you think you are? Given the people in this group, position yourself in relation to the others in this room. The higher you place yourself, the more religious you feel you are in relation to them. The lower you go, the less religious. (Expect people to stand on chairs and lie on the floor.)

> Are the traditional mitzvot important to the kind of Jewish life you would like to lead? One end of the room is designated for those who do not find the mitzvot important for them. The other end is for those who do find it important. Place yourself in the appropriate position, at either extreme of the room or anyplace in between.

> Is being Jewish central to your life? If so, stand at the designated point in the center of the room. Is it peripheral? Stand at the outer edges. Or, put yourself at any other place between the center and the edges that seems appropriate to your stance.

> For whom is Jewish communal life central? Peripheral? For whom is Jewish religious life central, etc.? Position yourself accordingly.

> How central is God to your life? Central? Go to the center of the room. Peripheral? Go to the periphery of the room.

> Are you more or less Jewish than your parents? Like your parents? Go to the middle of the room. Unlike them? Go to the edges.

> Are you more like or unlike the other people in this room?

Once people have positioned themselves and had a chance to look around, let them talk about why they are where they are. Take note of the shifts individuals make from question to question and have them discussed within the total group or in pairs.

A TEACHERS' TRAINING WORKSHOP BASED ON PREVIOUS THREE EXERCISES

Double Circles

1. Introduce yourself to the person in front of you. If you already know that person, introduce something new about yourself your partner probably doesn't know.
2. Is there anything you think you should know more about that would make you a better professional? If so, what?
3. What are some of the things you like about your job?
4. What are some of the things you don't like about your job?
5. What is likely to be a significant strength for you as a Jewish professional?
6. What is likely to be a significant weakness for you as a Jewish professional?
7. Would you like a child or other family member you treasure to join your profession?

Hillel Says:

What is most important to you as a Jew, what do you most want to communicate as a Jewish educator? Tell it to your group, but only while you stand on one foot.

People-grams:

Consider two poles of Jewish education. *There are people who feel*

1. That it is appropriate to think of a student as an empty tcacup and a teacher as a full pitcher whose task is to fill that cup.
2. That content is the most important thing in a Jewish education.
3. That without law and order in the classroom, learning cannot take place.
4. That it is the educational system and not the student that should determine what ought to be taught.

And then there are those who believe

1. That it is appropriate to think of a student as a tender seedling that will grow into its full potential if nurtured properly, and that a teacher is like a gardener whose task is to keep down the weeds and let the sun and the water help it grow.

2. That sufficient discipline will come of itself if students are learning what seems important to them.

3. That a reasonable amount of hubbub in the classroom does not get in the way of education, particularly if students are learning happily.

4. A student's own curiosity leads to the only kind of education that will stick. What the school decides is good for the student is irrelevant in the long run.

If we are to view those two sets of positions as polar extremes and designate each end of the room as one of them, where would you place yourself on the continuum?

Let us now talk about why you are where you have placed yourself and what that means for Jewish education.

REVIEWING AN EXERCISE AND MOVING ON

As in the case of Double Circles, you can defuse things by having a general meeting immediately afterwards. Ask:

> What happened?
>
> How did things go?
>
> Did anything happen that you want to share?

Don't belabor, don't overdo. You won't be able to get away with such a discussion at the end of every exercise, but if you do so at the end of the first few, you help people get into the swing of things. At the same time you will be able to see more clearly what is going on. You will want to have a general evaluation at the end, as a final wrap-up, so don't have so many discussions along the way that people become resistant to the process.

For such a discussion, you may need to assemble the participants in one place, or you may want to leave them where they are. Do whatever seems easiest and most natural.

A good way to shift from exercise to exercise is to have people move back and forth from pairs to groups of six. In this way they both build individual bonds out of the pairings and enjoy intimate small-group experiences. If you have pairs doing an exercise, you may want to suggest that for the next stage people get into groups of six to discuss how it went. Moving people in and out of the various groupings enables them to meet more and more members of the total group. In all cases, the flow should be as smooth as you can make it. One discussion should lead into the other with a minimum of confusion or unnecessary regrouping. You should develop a script, not only for each exercise, but from one exercise to the next.

A JEWISH SHOW-AND-TELL

(FOR PARENTS AND CHILDREN GRADES 1–3)

For our meeting, would each of you, children and parent/s, bring a Jewish Something and be prepared to tell the rest of us about it?

> Where did it come from?
>
> What do you do with it, or is just having it enough?
>
> Why is it important to you?"

When they come together, assemble in a circle and share. This is not a profound exercise, but it does provide some gentle conversation between parents and their young children.

WHAT IS YOUR JEWISH SECRET?

(FROM SHERRY ISRAEL)

Your instructions to the group:

> What is there about being Jewish that embarrasses you, that you dislike, that makes you ashamed, that you generally don't tell others? Without putting your name on the paper, write out your secret. We will then put the papers into the bowl in the center of the circle and read and discuss them.

This exercise requires a group that is large enough to preserve the anonymity of the secrets and small enough to allow a reading that will not take too long. A good number is fifteen to thirty. The discussion that follows will take the better part of an evening. To do it well, a warm-up is useful, and Double Circles will do the job. Be sure that people know that the secrets will be read publicly before you ask them to write anything down. They will censor themselves and avoid writing anything that will make them too uncomfortable.

RAMBAM SAYS

(FROM JOEL ZIFF)

This exercise offers a way to discuss tzedakah in groups of six to eight. Give participants a sheet with Maimonides' Eight Degrees of Charity on page 31 out of sequence, every which way, in random fashion. Ask each individual to rank them one to eight. Then bring people together and ask them if, as a group, they can rank the statements in order of priority. It is easy to do the beginning and the end of the list. The middle is harder. Have them compare and discuss each other's feelings about tzedakah. Why do they put the statements in the sequence they do?

MAIMONIDES' EIGHT DEGREES OF CHARITY

(ACCORDING TO HIS ORDER)

1. The who gives grudgingly, reluctantly, or with regret.
2. The one who gives less than is appropriate, but gives graciously.
3. The one who gives what is asked but only after being asked.
4. The one who gives before being asked.
5. The one who gives without knowing to whom the gift is given although the recipient knows the identity of the donor.
6. The one who gives anonymously.
7. The one who gives without knowing to whom the gift has been given, nor does the recipient know from whom the gift comes.
8. The one who helps a person to become self-supporting through a gift or a loan or by finding employment.

MAIMONIDES' EIGHT DEGREES OF CHARITY

The one who gives before being asked.

The one who gives without knowing to whom the gift is given although the recipient knows the identity of the donor.

The one who gives anonymously.

The who gives grudgingly, reluctantly, or with regret.

The one who helps a person to become self-supporting through a gift or a loan or by finding employment.

The one who gives what is asked but only after being asked.

The one who gives less than is appropriate, but gives graciously.

The one who gives without knowing to whom the gift has been given, nor does the recipient know from whom the gift comes.

PERSONALIZING MITZVOT

(FROM JOEL ZIFF)

Confluent learning theory holds that conceptual material can be taught more effectively and be most easily retained if what is being taught is applied directly to the life of the individual learner. The teaching of mitzvot is particularly appropriate to its methodology. A few examples may serve to show how this method may be used. Each of these illustrations may serve as the basis of a discussion in class or at a workshop or retreat. Whether the discussion takes place in pairs, in small groups, or in a large group depends on the setting, the tone, the participants, and their experience.

The fall holidays are not well distributed; they all seem to come at one time. They are a sort of stew. They all blend into one another with common themes, while at the same time, individual pieces retain their own individual qualities. *Rosh ha-Shanah* is described as the world's birthday. It calls attention to the theme of renewal, getting a fresh start, setting new goals. Even plants have done what they have done for the year and are now starting to gather strength for the next season.

What kind of birthday presents does the world need?

On *Rosh ha-Shanah* it is the custom to eat foods whose names make puns with the themes of the holidays. Traditionally these puns are in Hebrew or Yiddish, but they could be in English as well. For example: May only good things turnip for us, may we turnip new ways to live with enthusiasm. May our hearts beet for joy, may we beet down our inclination to sin. On jalapeño jelly—may He keep us out of hot jams.

Are there any other foods that could be used to express your feelings about the holiday?

The *Shofar* is said to serve as the year's alarm clock, arousing those aspects of our lives that have become numb and unresponsive. It declares the arrival of the Jubilee when debts are remitted, slaves freed, and land returned. The *Shofar* offers a new lease on life.

What aspect of your life needs to be awakened by the *Shofar?*

Shabbat Shuvah, the Shabbat in-between, may well be an appropriate day for a group to reflect on general directions in which it is going.

Yom Kippur is a day for accepting our responsibilities and trying to live accordingly. We ought not try to escape from them. This is why we read the Book of Jonah: he tried to get out of his responsibilities but did not succeed.

> What would you like to get away from, knowing full well that sooner or later you are going to have to do it?

Sukkot has two distinct themes: the commemoration of the years of wandering in the wilderness, and a festival of thanksgiving for the good things produced by the earth. There are three important elements of the celebration of the holiday: dwelling in the *sukkah*, acquiring and using *lulav* and *etrog,* and rejoicing.

As a it is symbol of thanksgiving, it is appropriate to decorate the *sukkah* attractively. A *sukkah* has to be more than three feet tall and less than thirty feet. It has to have at least two walls and part of a third, which can be made of most anything (except a dead camel). The essence of a *sukkah* is its *skakh*. (You can hear the relationship of the words.) Anything of which a vessel could reasonably be made cannot be used for *skakh*, thus eliminating metal and plastic. A *sukkah* is a rather organic structure. It is a frail structure suggesting the fragility of life. The *skakh* therefore may not be permanent. One who has to be in a *sukkah* is vulnerable to the vagaries of nature, and thus one should be able to see the stars through the *skakh*, which is why a *sukkah* may not be built under anything else, like a building or a tree. Nor may anything hang under the *skakh* aside from decorations (no supportive nets). The *sukkah* is frail, but because it is relatively open, the wind can generally blow against it without blowing it over.

> Are there aspects of your life that appear frail but may be less frail than they seem to be? A *sukkah* is not a *sukkah* if it is under a tree. What would cause you to lose your identity?

Ushpizin is the prayer welcoming the ancient leaders of Israel into our *sukkah. Sukkot* is a time to have guests.

> Who are the guests you would want in your *sukkah*? Why? Any historical guests? What kind of world would we see through their eyes?

Lulav and *etrog* can be thought of as teaching devices: The *lulav* and *etrog,* agricultural products of Israel, are used as symbols of our gratitude for what the land yields. The *lulav* is made of branches of palm, myrtle, and willow. The *etrog* is a citron. (Plant the seeds after *Sukkot* and you will have little trees for your kids by *Tu Bish'vat.*)

They can also be construed as metaphors: The *lulav* and *etrog* are sometimes interpreted as referring to four kinds of Jews. The *etrog* has both taste and aroma and represents Jews with learning and deeds. The palm's dates have taste but no aroma and represent Jews who have learning but no deeds. The Myrtle has no taste but has aroma and represents Jews who have no learning but who perform deeds. The willow, finally, has neither taste nor aroma and represents those Jews who have neither learning nor deeds.

	Deeds vs.	Learning
Etrog	taste &	smell
Myrtle	0	smell
Palm	taste	0
Willow	0	0

What aspects of you are described by this rubric? What are your strengths and lackings in learning and deeds? In what ways does your particular mix make you special? What would you lose without them?

In another metaphor, the *lulav* and *etrog* are described as being like a person:

Etrog = Heart	Myrtle = Eyes
Palm = Spine	Willow = Lips

Make up your own exercise. What are the questions you might ask about the *lulav* and *etrog* or the *sukkah* that might both instruct people about the holidays and ask them to reflect upon their lives?

One is not limited to the holidays to use this approach: Tzedakah and its priorities are described in the exercise *Rambam Says* (p. __).

What about your own practice of tzedakah? Are you satisfied with your own conduct? To what extent do you live according to the priorities you say you believe to be important?

Tefillin, placed on the head and the arm, directly over the heart, are often described as activating and clarifying important sources of power related to your use of your head, your hands, or your heart.

Are you a hands person or a head person? How will you use each type of power in your life today? How can each type of energy enhance the others? In what ways do they act in opposition?

GOD GAMES

(FROM LAWRENCE KUSHNER, WHO ADAPTED IT FROM ZALMAN SCHACHTER)

Kushner says that if he asks people to tell whether they believe in God, almost no one admits to such belief, but if he asks about their experiences with God, almost everyone has something to report.

God Games are about those reports. They are a device to give people a way to talk about their religious feelings and aspirations. They are usually there if we can help them speak without embarrassment. When people discover that others too have had these experiences, they are helped and encouraged to play additional "games" with God. If people have absolutely empty *neshomas* (souls), there may be nothing we can do, but I suspect that few are in that condition.

Start by telling a story. The most suitable ones usually turn out to be Hasidic tales in which one of the figures is engaged in an important, though possibly playful, relationship with God. Examples of tales for *God Games* would include Y.L. Peretz's "If Not Higher" and the Levi Yitzhak stories. *A Treasury of Jewish Folklore,* by Nathan Ausubel (Crown Publishing, New York, 1948), contains many such stories, particularly the sections on "Holy Men" and "Miracles".

You may want to offer a few comments or raise some questions about the story. If you use the Peretz story or the Levi Yitzhak stories, you might ask:

> What was the Rabbi of Nemirov's relation to God?
>
> Was he merely doing social work?
>
> What was the Litvak's relationship?
>
> In the story about the tailor who could have brought the Messiah, does Levi Yitzhak really believe that God can be manipulated?
>
> What relationship to God does this story imply?
>
> Do we seek such intimacy or think it is possible?

Keep the discussion brief or you will find yourself stuck in literary analysis. Your introduction to the substance of the activity might go like this:

> "Many of us have had some expectations that something would happen in a relationship with God,—i.e., we have tried to play

games with God. What I should like to do now is encourage you to talk about one of the *God Games* you have played. Has anything religious happened to you that was really important? Did you ever want such a thing to happen? Tell the story in the third person: He or she did these things or had these thoughts. Talk about it as if you were telling a story relating an event that happened to someone else, as in the story we just heard. The third-person formulation makes it much easier to talk. It provides a measure of distance from the material. Talk about it with a person in the group you don't know well."

This last instruction may be unnecessary if by this time in your program people in subgroups have developed enough intimacy to sustain such a discussion in that larger setting.

Allow fifteen or twenty minutes of discussion to pass. Then ask participants to tell another story about a game they would like to have played with God. Once again, have them cast it in the third person, as if it happened to someone else.

Finally, the setting for the last story:

"Your death is very near. What kind of game would you like to play with God then? Tell the story."

You may want to precede the games or follow them with a study of certain texts from the Midrash or tales from Jewish folklore, for they are often the record of the *God Games* of another generation.

OBITUARIES

To deal with the question of what we want to be, do, have, or experience before it's all over, ask the participants to write out their own obituaries for the local paper and then discuss them. If you don't want them to write, a more brief oral form of this exercise is to have people formulate the inscriptions for their tombstones.

A variation of this theme is to write out ethical wills. To get them started, read aloud, or have the participants read, some examples from *Hebrew Ethical Wills*, Abrahams, I. (J.P.S., Philadelphia, 1976), *Shaarei Mitzvah—Gates of Mitzvah* (C.C.A.R., New York, 1977), or *So That Your Values Live On*, Riemer, J. and Stampfir, N. (Jewish Lights Publishing, Woodstock, Vermont, 1991).

DAYS OF AWE

During the High Holiday season, *Selihot*, *Shabbat Shuvah*, or the afternoon of *Yom Kippur*, variations on the following exercise may be of help:

Start with Double Circles (see *Pre-Yom Kippur Workshop*, p. 18). Open with the positive formulation,—i.e., "What did you do well?" before "Whom did you hurt?" Ask for the high points of the year before the low ones. Use "What do you look forward to during the coming year?" before "What relationships are you likely to botch?"

Next, do the obituaries or tombstone inscriptions. Be sure to allow enough time for discussion.

These exercises can provide an important forum in which people can share their aspirations and grow from doing so. I have found that many people save their obituaries for years to come as a kind of document to live by.

You should be extremely careful about the manner in which you get people into these exercises. Be sure they want to be there. Do not intrude on their life space without their assent. It is not easy to do these exercises in a large crowd or congregation, where many people come on the assumption that they will be able to preserve their anonymity. I do not suggest them as part of a regular service, but rather for those who might want to stay around after the service. You may want a helper to move about and encourage people or groups that are bogged down.

A note of caution: From time to time Hillel directors or rabbis in small congregations have organized into workshops after the end of services on *Kol Nidre* evening. Reports of experiences at three different places lead me to advise strongly against this. Under the best of circumstances souls frayed by Yom Kippur have a difficult time, and it comes as no surprise to learn that these workshops have from time to time elicited straightforward psychotic behavior. Not only did disturbed people have to be quieted down, but the experience proved to be traumatic for the others who were present. It is hard to determine whether the workshops generated such behavior or whether people in profound difficulty gravitated to them, but it makes no difference. Unless you want major problems, do the usual liturgical thing on *Kol Nidre*. The service is powerful enough to carry itself. The only exception to this rule would be if the service is for a small community you know well and feel confident about.

OTHER DISCUSSION POSSIBILITIES FOR LITURGICAL SETTINGS

FOR A PASSOVER SEDER:

When did you personally leave Egypt, or when would you like to? (from Joseph Polak)

What kind of baggage would you bring with you? What would you leave behind?

What is one of your earliest Seder memories? (The older the people, the better the answers.)

Tell about one of your important Seder memories. (from Bernard Pucker)

FOR SHABBAT:

How do each of the Kabbalat Shabbat psalms relate to each of the days of your past week? Reflect upon this theme as you go over them in the siddur. Your thoughts can be shared or just reflected upon. (from Joseph Polak)

A SHABBAT "MEAL"

This is an experimental, non-traditional worship experience for those who want to pray but do not find themselves satisfied with normative liturgies. It is suitable for eight to twenty people and is based on the Sabbath meal rather than the *Kabbalat Shabbat* liturgy. It takes the following form:

1. Candles are lit beforehand. They are the only light in the room. *Hallot* on a plate are on the floor between the candles, along with a large cup of *Kiddush* wine.

2. Sit quietly on the floor in a circle as people come in.

3. *Shalom Aleichem* is sung quietly.

4. *Vay'khulu* is read in English. *Kiddush* is sung in Hebrew. The cup is passed around, and everyone drinks.

5. Content: A story, a poem, or perhaps some readings. The participants are encouraged to offer their own "gifts"—readings or thoughts that are important to them. Someone may bring a flower.

    Look at a rose until you see it in all of its uniqueness. Look at a daisy until it can be seen in its connectedness with all of life. See it in its contiguity with all creation rather than its discreteness. Have a fantasy about the world immediately after the creation was finished. Imagine what was on the other side of the *Sambatyon*. Sometimes quiet discussion is in order.

6. *N'tilat yadayim*, with each person washing the hands of the next one, using a massive cup, bowl, and towel.

7   *Ha-Motzi* by the leader (Hebrew and English). Loaves are passed around. Each person breaks off a piece of *hallah.* Slowly savor it; don't just gobble it up.

8. A period of silence.

9. A *niggun* (wordless melody) sung quietly.

10. A one-line *Birkat ha-Mazon.*

The service lasts about forty-five minutes, with much silence between the segments. It is essential that the setting be a quiet one without disturbance.

JEWISH SURVIVAL GAME

(FROM STEPHEN & EVA ROBBINS)

Have participants make individual lists of the ten items they would bring with them to a desert island that would maximize the likelihood of their survival as Jews. Then discuss the lists jointly. Try to arrive at a common list. Allow thirty to sixty minutes.

TIME CAPSULE

(FROM FRAN GINSBERG)

This is a device to get people to discuss the American Jewish experience. In groups of six to twelve have the group imagine that they are opening a time capsule put away by the Jewish communities of 1920, 1950, or 1970.

> What are the characteristic artifacts that would most likely have been put in?

> What objects would have offered insight into that particular period of Jewish life?

Discuss the periods one at a time, or if there are enough participants, discuss different time periods in different groups. As you go along make lists of the artifacts on a blackboard or on large sheets of paper. With luck the discussion that will accompany the listing of those objects will be a good reflective discussion of what each period was all about. The presence of a few older participants in this discussion will help.

The same exercise can be used for any other period of Jewish life.

I AM

Have each participant write out a list of ten words or phrases, each completing the statement "I am . . ."

Have them share lists with pair partners. After the pairs have spoken for a few minutes, ask them to deal with this question:

> Where does the term Jew appear on the list, and why is it located where it is?

TEN JEWISH THINGS

This activity, suitable for up to a hundred people and lasting 30–50 minutes, is a good mixer or an introduction to later activities. It can also be used to gather people into Double Circles. In the latter case, some people will have to be shifted about in order to even up groups. Give the following instructions.

Fold or make a line down the center of a piece of paper. Make a plus (+) mark at the head of one column, a minus (-) mark at the head of the other.

In the first column list ten things associated with Jews, Judaism, and being Jewish with which you have a positive association.

Now, in the second column, list ten negative items you associate with Jews, Judaism, and being Jewish.

Star the most positive and most negative items.

Pin the list on yourself and then, on the basis of the starred items, go find a person or group of people with a set of Jewish values that is similar to yours. When you find such a person or people, sit down with them and discuss your lists.

YOUR JEWISH VALUES

First individually, and then in small groups, rank the following items in what you believe to be their order of importance, with "1" being the most important, "2" second most important, etc. Allow about half an hour for discussion, then compare group results. If you want to score the exercise, add up the numbers on the individual pages within a group. Lowest-scored items are considered most important.

Israel's survival

A warm, supportive mate

The Jewish religious tradition

Being healthy

Not intermarrying

Giving tzedakah

World peace

Financial security

JEWISH MEMORIES

(FROM BERNARD REISMAN)

1. What is your most recent Jewish memory (the last Jewish thing you did)?
2. What is your earliest Jewish memory?
3. What is your most important Jewish memory?
4. What kind of Jewish memories would you like your children to have?
5. How can you help that to happen? Will it require a change in your life?

Allow time between questions for discussion in pairs or in groups of four to six. For each question allocate three to five minutes to each person in the group.

If you do this exercise with people who are too young, they may not have Jewish memories that are sufficiently significant to build on. I have found this exercise difficult with high school students; it has almost never failed with adults. Success with college students is uneven. The older they are, the more likely the exercise will work.

PASSOVER PAST, PASSOVER PRESENT

KEEPING JEWISH MEMORIES ALIVE

This exercise is a variation on the previous one. It could be adapted for use as well with other holidays or Jewish life-cycle events. It may be done either in Double Circles or in a small group. I find this particular set of questions useful as part of a workshop to prepare people for conducting a seder.

1. What is your earliest Passover memory?
2. What is the most memorable thing that ever happened to you at Passover?
3. Is there any story that you can tell from your past, either from a seder or from some other aspect of the Jewish life of your family that would help your children understand you better?
4. What kind of stories were they?
5. Are they stories you could tell at your seder?

IMPORTANT JEWISH EVENTS

(FROM BERNARD REISMAN)

This exercise for ten to fifty people attempts to help participants focus on their differing perceptions of Jewish history and to notice how these perceptions condition their Jewish life-styles and activities. Before the game starts, take five large sheets of paper and write one of the following on each:

The giving of the Torah and the Exodus

The destruction of the Temples and subsequent life in the Diaspora

The American Jewish experience

The destruction of the European Jewish community

The establishment of the State of Israel

Put these aside. Begin the exercise by asking participants to write their choices for the most important single event in Jewish history on a piece of paper. When they have finished, hang up your five sheets of paper. Events chosen usually cluster around these categories. Solicit people's choices and write their formulation on the appropriate sheets.

When your lists are complete, ask them to assemble under the list on which their selection appears. Have the members of each group discuss why they joined that group. Then have discussion between the groups.

A VISIT TO THE HOME FOR THE AGED

This exercise is intended to build bridges between two groups of a very different character. It works well, for example, with high-school or college students and the residents of a home for the aged. In mixed groups of six:

Introduce yourself.

Talk about your home.

How do you spend your day?

Talk about something good that has happened to you and something bad that has happened to you.

Allow ten to fifteen minutes for discussion between questions. When the discussion is over one or both groups can provide some entertainment and refreshments.

In a home for the aged, the students will learn a great deal about old people, how they spend their time, and what their concerns are. The old people will learn as well. There will be little patronizing since everyone has a day to talk about and also highs and lows to share. The students will gain understanding even if the answer to "How do you spend your day?" is "I get up in the morning and have nothing to do."

I have also found this exercise effective with a group of migrant farm workers and upper-middle-class Jewish high school students.

WARRING CAMPS

This is a negotiating workshop for two disparate groups that don't particularly like each other: traditionalists and secularists in the same Hillel foundation, parents and children, perhaps even rabbis and their congregants. It is suitable for twenty-five to fifty people. Antagonists may vary from setting to setting.

Assume that we are dealing with students and parents. For a warm-up use the Double Circles questions from A Parent-Child Interchange (p. __) with the total group.

The "Warring Camps" then go to opposite sides of a large room, each with a staff member. Give each group a big sheet of paper and a marker.

The first question for the parents' group:

What is right about your kids?

For the students' group:

What is right about your parents?

Get one person in each group, preferably not the staff member, to be a non-censoring recorder. Have the recorder write down everything the group wishes. The groups don't need to spend more than eight minutes on this first list. Then start a second list:

What is wrong about parents? (for the students' list)

What is wrong about students? (for the parents' list)

This will take more time. At first they may be reluctant to put anything negative on the list. They may even need a bit of staff encouragement: "Is that really all you find wrong?" However, they will warm to their task and generate some surprisingly long negative lists with great enthusiasm. After a while they may become concerned that they have been too extreme. If the situation is sufficiently tense, you may want to go right to the bone and ask only for the "what is wrong" list, though I prefer to include both. The use of the positive list seems to get them into the negative list with greater gusto. The groups remain apart but within earshot. They will be goaded on by the hilarity they hear emerging from the opposite end of the room. When they run out of items, take each chart to the other group. Its exhibition will also become an occasion for great mirth and merriment.

The next assignment:

What might you have done to contribute to that image and to have given the others such an impression of you? Much of the problem may have to do with the insensitivity of the other group, but what is your responsibility in the matter? You must surely have some. List your contributions to the problem.

Finally, bring everyone together. People have been having a lot of fun. They will be in a good humor and deeply involved in the issues, and will probably be able to succeed with a role play. Identify some of the issues that are really aggravating to both groups. Have a member from one group talk to one from the other in front of the total group about an issue or incident that separates them.

Don't get bogged down in theory or trivia. What are the gut-level things that truly disturb them? Kids may be angry about parents dominating their lives. Parents may be angry about their children's irresponsibility. The traditionalists may be convinced that the non-traditionalists are Jewishly ignorant and not to be taken seriously, whereas the liberals and secularists may be sick of patronizing or downright negative attitudes on the part of the traditionalists. Pick a concrete example—an actual, recent incident, if possible—that illustrates the problem (e.g., lighting candles after sunset on Friday evening) and have two people try to work it through. After they have been at it for a while, and as soon as you sense they are about to become repetitious, ask the onlookers from the two groups to comment.

This will be more than a whole program. People will have a good time. They will feel better about their counterparts because you have validated the legitimacy of their own positions. Once they know that they have been heard, they will feel better about the others.

JEWS AND CHRISTIANS

This is an interfaith activity for mixed groups of six to twelve.

Ask participants to write down the first ten words or phrases they associate with the term "Jew." When they have finished, have them turn their papers over (or make a second column) and write down their first ten associations with the term "Christian." There is nothing special about the number ten; some of the participants may not be able to complete their lists.

After the lists are written, have the participants share them with one another, either orally or by trading papers. They should then discuss the lists and their reactions to them. The entire exercise takes about an hour.

You might want to point out an interesting theme that frequently emerges. In the English language, when you say to a person: "You have behaved like a Jew," you have probably insulted that person; when you say: "You behaved like a Christian," you have paid the person a compliment. Is anti–Semitism built into Western culture?

CLAY

The instructions for Clay:

> Choose a partner and form that person into a statue, posing it however you wish.

> The person being formed is asked to hold whatever pose the sculptor creates. After all of the statues are finished, have a brief exhibit so that the sculptors can see one another's work. Then the partners switch roles; sculptors become clay, and the statues become sculptors.

Some of the sculptors will be mean and put the others into positions that are uncomfortable and hard to hold (often dancers trying to show off their suppleness). You may want to warn people that they will be changing roles; this will restrain most of them, for they won't want the others to get even with them. Some of the poses will be artful, some obscene, some hostile, some awkward. The range is truly impressive. At the end of the exercise, if you like, ask people to mechanize their statues and turn them on. That adds a touch of fun with no significant dimension.

This exercise involves touching of a nonthreatening sort, which usually creates some intimacy and a general feeling that people are able to relax with one another. Such a mood makes it easier to discuss the psychosexual issues raised in the next two games, though it can stand on its own as a mixer without them. It can be done with grade-school age on up. The next two are only for older groups.

MAKE A GESTURE

A good exercise to follow *Clay* is:

Make a male gesture (both members of the sculpting pair).

Make a female gesture (again, both of them).

Talk about it with your partner.

The couple will have a lot to talk about, chiefly stereotyping, but also their own particular understanding of the "typical" behavior of men and women.

In this exercise you may want people to report to the total group those experiences that might be of interest. Don't force those who don't want to to report, but be sure to allow reporting as an option. This exercise may engender some anxiety that people will want to defuse.

SHAMMAI SAYS

(FROM YEHIEL POUPKO)

If you do *Clay* followed by *Make a Gesture*, and things are going well, you can get into *Shammai Says* without much difficulty. This exercise will encourage some first-rate discussion, with Jewish overtones, on important issues of sexual identity. It should be used with caution since it requires a group in which people can talk about such matters without getting silly. It should be used in a situation in which participants feel that they can take risks without being excessively nervous. Still in pairs, the partners work with each other.

The instructions are:

Put your hands on the part of your body that commits the most sins.

Put your hands on the part of your body that commits the fewest sins.

Put your hands on the part of your body that wants to commit more sins.

Put your hands on the part of your body that wants to commit the fewest sins.

Put your hands on the part of your body that is the holiest.

Put your hands on the part of your body that is the least holy.

Put your hands on the part of your body that will get to the Holy Land first when the Messiah comes.

If you can get that far, the participants will have a lot to talk about. Give them the time. The exercise can certainly be used in mixed groups, but only if you as a leader feel more relaxed about using it. It is an exercise that is both powerful and fun.

If the discussion goes in the direction of the messianic issue, you might ask:

What would you bring along at the final Redemption to show the Messiah that you are Jewish?

What would you want to have with you in the World to Come?

AN EVENING OF MOSTLY NONVERBAL INTRODUCTIONS

Consider this series of exercises as a substitute for a mixer. Be sure to advertise it accurately so that no one is misled. It may also be used for a "captive" group as long as you make it clear that people do not have to participate when they do not feel comfortable doing so (see *Further Cautionary Notes*, p. 90).

1. Get the feel of your body:

   Close your eyes and direct your attention to your breath, your heartbeat, the temperature of the air. Can you smell anything? What can you hear?

   (Note to the leader: Give this exercise a little more time than you might think is required. If people fall asleep, you have gone too long.)

2. To loosen bodies:

   Lie on the floor; stretch, relax. Exaggerate your breathing. Fill your body with air as if you were a balloon. Imagine filling your toes, your fingers, your arms, your legs; then suddenly you collapse, letting it all out. Try a second time. Whom can you reach and touch from where you are lying on the floor?

   Form a group of five or six to share your feelings about what happened. Pick people who are in the vicinity. Hold hands with your group of six with eyes closed; move in whatever way feels natural. Stand up slowly. Continue to hold hands with eyes closed and see what happens to the motion of the group. Then move slowly through space.

3. Milling about (no talking throughout the exercise):

   Mill about first with eyes opened. Now you are in Grand Central Station. Move about rapidly, trying not to touch anyone. Go into slow motion, then normal speed. When your eyes lock with those of someone else, approach each other and nonverbally introduce yourselves. Continue milling about, eyes closed. After you get used to this, explore the faces of those you bump into (eyes still closed). Open eyes; mill about once again. Find someone to walk with. Match the other person's stride with yours. What does it feel like to walk with another? Change partners.

4. Competition, collaboration, and leadership:

   Pick partners. Standing and facing your partner, place your upright palms against your partner's and push. Do the same thing with several people. Talk about it. Who tried to push partners over? Who took account of partner's strength and held back? Talk about how it felt. Pick a new partner. Place your feet together, put your toes touching your partner's. Take hold of your partner's hands, lean back, put arms out full length, and balance each other by forming an inverted triangle. With arms held out and toes together, can you bend your knees to a squat and then stand again? You will have to trust your partner in order to do this. Exchange partners several times and talk about it.

   Sit cross-legged in front of a partner; let one partner move hands slowly and the other follow as if in a mirror. Pass the leadership back and forth until you can't tell who is leading. Slow music helps but is not essential. Talk about how it felt.

5. Group sculpture:

   One person starts by holding a pose and becoming the first part of a sculpture. Then the next person assumes a pose which touches the body of the first person and, when settled, also freezes into position. As many people as want to join in. You may want to suggest a theme for the sculpture. Let the sculpture come to life and perhaps turn into a machine. Consider having two separate sculptures become two separate machines that then have to work together. Consider making a "group typewriter." It is great fun.

6. Conclusion:

   Sit in a circle and hold hands. Hum a little. The leader makes a gesture or a motion which is then passed along with the hands through the total group. Break into groups of five or six. Let each take five minutes to tell the others their Jewish spiritual biographies. Be sure that there is enough time for everyone.

ORGANIZATIONAL AND INSTITUTIONAL EXERCISES

INTERVIEWS

The interview sheet is a way to start a program before it officially begins. The sheets can be passed out on the bus on the way to the event or placed in registration kits as people begin to arrive for a weekend gathering. Ask participants to fill out the sheets by interviewing someone they don't know. Ask them to bring the forms to the next public gathering, where they will be collected and (with permission from the interviewees) posted with tape around the walls.

This sheet gives each participant at least one new friend at a gathering of strangers. Furthermore, it legitimates the appropriateness of talking about feelings from the very beginning. A suggested format appears on the following page.

INTERVIEW SHEET

We invite you to interview another participant at this gathering. The interviewing process assumes that everyone here brings something to this event that is worth sharing. This is a place to record some of those things. Please take time to interview someone you don't know. That person will then interview you. This helps us to link people together on the basis of needs, skills, and interests.

1. If you divided the way you spend your time into three segments, how would you describe these segments, and in what order, based on time spent, would you place them?

   a.

   b.

   c.

2. What three adjectives would you use to describe yourself?

   a.

   b.

   c.

3. What is the most recent thing you have read?

4. Who are your heroes and/or heroines?

5. What are your hopes and/or expectations from this weekend?

6. What is the last Jewish thing you did or encountered?

7. Is there anything you could do or share at this weekend (talents, special interests others could learn about, etc.)?

8. Name_____

9. Interviewed by:_____

10. May this interview be posted? Yes___ No___

When it is completed, please give this form to staff member.

THE HELPING RELATIONSHIP

We are all called upon to "help" one another frequently. Few tasks are harder. The three sequenced exercises that follow will assist people to explore the nature of helping. Allow five minutes of discussion between each segment of the exercises and at the end.

HELPING RELATIONSHIP #1—INTRODUCTION

The exercise is done in pairs. The partners decide who is to be the client and who the consultant. Hand out copies of the puzzle ("The Anthropologist's Problem") to both the client and the consultant. Give the consultant the solution as well. Allow them ten to fifteen minutes to work with the puzzle, and then give the solution on the client. At that time both partners also get the discussion sheet.

HELPING RELATIONSHIP #1

THE ANTHROPOLOGIST'S PROBLEM

An anthropologist was lost in the jungles of Central America. He knew he was in the area of the two Answar (pronounce it *Anne's war*) tribes. Each member of the first tribe had an unusual red "birthmark" on his left foot. The members of that tribe *never* told the truth to strangers. The other tribe had no such mark. They *always* told the truth to strangers.

The anthropologist came upon three natives standing in a stream fishing. He knew it would insult the men to ask to see their feet. Nevertheless, he needed to know which man would give him accurate directions.

He asked the first man, "Have you any mark on your left foot?"

The man responded in a sign language (he was mute) which the anthropologist could not understand. He knew, however, that the other natives did understand the sign, and he asked the second man, "What did he say?"

"He said that he has a red mark on his left foot," replied the second man.

The anthropologist turned to the third man and asked, "Did the second man tell the truth?"

"No," replied the third man. From this the anthropologist knew which man to trust. How did he know?

HELPING RELATIONSHIP #1

THE ANTHROPOLOGIST'S PROBLEM—A SOLUTION

Because all the tribesmen with birthmarks never told the truth, it is impossible, by the facts given, for any tribesman to say "I have a red mark on my left foot." Those who do have a red mark lie and *say they do not*. Those who do not have a red mark tell the truth and *say they do not*.

Accordingly, the second man lied when he told the anthropologist that the first man said that he had such a mark. If the second man lied, the third told the truth and could be trusted to give accurate directions.

No conclusions can be drawn about the first man.

Helping Relationship #1

Discussion Sheet

As you discuss what you just did, consider these questions together:

To the person being helped:

> Was the consultant helpful?
>
> Did the consultant lead you to discover it yourself?
>
> Which would you have preferred?
>
> How did it make you feel to be the one who did not have the answer? Challenged? Stupid? Angry? (etc.)

To the consultant:

> Did the person being helped want your help? Did you know what kind of help was wanted? (For instance, did the client want you to give clues or prefer that you wait for questions?)
>
> How did you give help? Did you listen to "where the client was" or plunge right in?
>
> How did it make you feel to be the one with the answer? Smart? Embarrassed? Glad? (etc.)

To both:

> Who decided what kind of help was to be given, the consultant or the person being helped?

HELPING RELATIONSHIP #2

A ROW OF HATS

The guests at a party played a game in which three men were seated in chairs, one behind the other. All the men faced the same direction. The last man could see the back of the heads of the two in front. The middle man could see only the head of the front man. The front man could not see either of the other two. They were not to turn around.

They were told that there were five party hats available: three white hats and two red hats. One hat was placed on the head of each of the three men.

The last man was asked, "What color is your hat?"

After some thought he said, "I don't know."

The middle man was asked the color of his hat. After some thought he also replied, "I don't know."

The front man, who could not see the other two, was asked the color of his hat and, after some thought, he gave the correct color.

How did he know the color of his hat?

A Row of Hats—A Solution

Had there been *two red* hats on the middle and front men, the last man would have known the color of his hat. Therefore, the two men in front of him must have been wearing either *two* white hats or *one red* and *one white*.

Had the front man been wearing a *red* hat the middle man would have known his to be white, but he did not know.

Accordingly, the front man must have been wearing a white hat, the only remaining alternative.

HELPING RELATIONSHIP #2

DISCUSSION SHEET

To the consultant:

> What is different about helping when you aren't sure you have the right answer?

To the person being helped:

> What is different when you aren't sure the helper has the right answer?

To both:

> What happened? Did you switch roles or revert to your previous roles?
>
> Did you cooperate in solving it? Did you work independently?
>
> Which situation is more like real life?
>
> How did it feel to be on the other side?
>
> Had you learned anything from the first puzzle exercise?

Helping Relationship #3

Introduction

The final segment of this exercise is done in groups of three. Two people will select for themselves roles as consultants. One will choose to be a client. Therefore each client will have two consultants.

Each of the clients should think of a short, concrete, organizational classroom situation or, if preferred, a non-institutional situation that the client would like to be able to handle better. The client will provide the consultants with information about the setting and the characters as well as any other information they might need to understand the situation. The description should take no more than five minutes. The consultants should each take up to five minutes, one after the other, in order to consult and be as helpful as they can.

Distribute the instructions to the appropriate people, making sure that the consultants do not read one another's material until the exercise is concluded.

Allow ten minutes at the end for discussion.

Helping Relationship #3

Instructions For Consultant "Reuven"

Be yourself. There are many occasions in life when people ask for your advice and assistance. Do whatever you would normally do under such circumstances. Follow the style with which you feel most comfortable.

As you work with your "client" make mental notes of any problems you encounter. Does the client really want help? Do you feel that the client accepts what you have to offer?

During the five minutes when you are the non-active consultant, listen to and observe the other consultant-client interaction as carefully as you can. You may need to provide feedback later on.

Helping Relationship #3

Instructions for Consultant "Shimon"

The other consultant is being asked to give advice in a "normal" fashion. When asked for advice, most people give it. In your consultation, don't. *Do not leap in! Maybe* you will have a few suggestions for your client at the end of the consultation, but your primary goal should be to understand the client and the client's problem, not solve it. You are trying to help the *client* come up with solutions to the problem. Don't grill the client with long questions. Sometimes the most helpful thing you can do is to help a person define the problem more clearly.

As you work with your "client" make mental notes of any problems you encounter. Does the client really want help? Do you feel that the client accepts what you have to offer?

During the five minutes when you are the non-active consultant, listen to and observe the other consultant-client interaction as carefully as you can. You may need to provide feedback later on.

AN ELECTION

This is a simple discussion about the nature of appropriate leadership. It is suitable for single or multiple groups of six to ten and should take approximately half an hour.

Have the members of the group read the election platforms that follow and then discuss their presidential choice. The most tempting resolution will be for them to say, "We would really like a combination of the two," and with that conclude the discussion. Don't let them off so quickly. The function of this exercise is to make them think out the issues between Ephraim and Menashe. The credentials of the candidates peg them at student age. If you are working with adults, you should work out a different and appropriate list of credentials. The main point is that one is to be "organizational" but not "Jewish" and the other is to be "Jewish" but not "organizational." As you go along you might ask some questions. These two will prove useful if the group swings in the direction of Ephraim.

> What kind of a Jewish future would Ephraim offer us? What about Menashe?

> Is Jewish religious culture or organizational culture more likely to survive? Do we care?

If they go in the direction of Menashe, the following may be in order:

> Are belief and commitment sufficient for contemporary Jewish leadership?

> If Menashe had real Jewish commitment, wouldn't he have been involved in Jewish organizational life as well? Can you be a committed Jew and not be involved in the community?

> What are your chances of educating either one in some of the skills of the other?

At the end of the discussion take a vote. Don't be surprised if many refuse to vote. No matter. It is the discussion you care about.

TWO ELECTION PLATFORMS

Ephraim and Menashe have each been nominated for the presidency. Neither is an ideal candidate, but they are the only people who would accept the nominations. A summary of the speeches of each of them follows. Our responsibility (after a discussion of their qualifications) is to elect one of them.

EPHRAIM: I feel that I am well qualified to be the president of your group. I have had many years of organizational experience as president of my fraternity, vice-president of the drama club, and editor of our school paper. This past summer I was the leader of a group of students on a bicycle trip to famous cathedrals in France and was completely responsible for a group of twenty of my peers. Last year I was elected by the student council to represent our school at the White House Conference on Youth and was the youngest person from our area to go.

It is true that I have never been active in Jewish affairs, but then neither have my parents. I am not a very religious person. I hated Sunday school and do not regret that I dropped at an early age. My friends all assure me that I would only have learned nonsense there anyway.

I am interested in being president because I would like to stand up and be counted as a Jew and help my fellow Jews. I would not have felt this way had I not successfully worked through an experience with an anti–Semitic member of my bicycle tour group. I am still not very enthusiastic about Jewish culture, but even though I am a latecomer I want to work for a Jewish group. I have the kind of organizational background that should give me the ability to be an effective president.

MENASHE: Unlike Ephraim, I have no organizational experience. I would like to run for the presidency of our organization because I think that we should stand for Jewish values.

I have gone through Jewish day school since kindergarten, and my experience there was wonderful. Whenever there was a really good teacher in the school I was somehow fortunate enough to be in that teacher's class. My parents, seeing how much I enjoyed Jewish studies, got me a tutor so that I could take extra lessons in Talmud. I learned enough from my tutors to be able to spend the past several summers at a yeshiva in Israel and found that I could keep up with the regular students quite easily. It goes without saying that I live according to Jewish tradition. Even now, here at school, I find a little time each day to study Gemara.

Actually, it is because of my interest in Jewish life that I have never been very active in Jewish organizations. It struck me that all that ever went on were dances and parties, and that the people who ran them were little more than politicians.

But now I see that someone has to step in and give things some real Jewish direction. I think that I would be that person. There should be *shiurim* and seminars. A *Shabbaton* should be planned that would involve serious commitment to Jewish study. Worship should not be something that just has to be gotten over with. We really have got to learn to *daven* properly. I would like to lead in a direction that would encourage our members to move toward such goals.

TEN COMMANDMENTS FOR A GROUP

If you had your way, what would be a list of ten values that this class/group/synagogue/center should run by? Is there such a set of ten commandments that we could all agree upon that could be an acceptable set of values for this community?

Write your own list and then share.

TEAM BUILDING

(ADAPTED FROM AN EXERCISE OF

NATIONAL TRAINING LABORATORIES)

This is an exercise for groups of five of six that creates what it illustrates, a warm, functioning group. Introduce the exercise by indicating that the participants will be given some topics to discuss in small groups. Their task as individuals will be to complete on paper some short sentences that you will give them. They will then discuss their responses to the sentences in their groups, with each discussion lasting seven or eight minutes. These topics are intended to draw people close to one another in ways that would happen with any group of people working together for a period of time.

At the end of each discussion stop the conversations by introducing the next question. At first a staff member may have to wander about helping the groups to stick to the topics.

When I first enter a new group I feel...

My greatest strength as a Jew is...

To me, being Jewish is...

If I intermarried, my family would...

What I am afraid is going to happen is...

The most difficult sort of person in my school/Hillel Foundation/youth group/synagogue, etc., is...

(Addressing another member of the small group): When you were eight years old, I imagine you were...

In this group I have felt...

You may want to add to or subtract from the question list depending on how the discussions are going. They usually go overtime, and cutting will be indicated. At the appropriate time stop the discussion and combine two or three groups. Continue now with several additional sentences to be discussed in the larger setting.

I feel closest to others when...

If I had to do it over again, I would...

The thing about me that I need to work on is...

In a large group I usually...

After ten minutes return the participants to the small circles. They will go eagerly. Have them talk about how they feel back again in their small circles. Then have them make a short list of the items that helped them to form a close team and feel at home in their small groups.

Hang some large sheets of paper on the wall that are headlined with what the fill-in sentences were intended to engender:

Talk about feelings

Sharing of some personal background with others

Discussion of the present

Trust and openness

Feedback

Enjoyment

Have them read off their small groups' lists while you write their items in the appropriate places in the large sheets you have hung on the wall. If the items they listed helped them build a warm team, how do their own "back-home" groups provide such experiences? Which of these elements are present back home? Which are lacking, and what can be done to remedy the deficiencies?

DECISION MAKING

This is an exercise for groups of six to twelve. It is not what it appears to be on the surface, a discussion of "Leadership Issues in Groups." In fact, it is a slightly rigged discussion starter that is used to illustrate the ways this particular group makes decisions. The participants will become very interested in the content, and it will be very hard to get them to stop talking about it. You, the facilitator or leader, are much more interested in the decision-making process.

The phrasing of each sentence in the exercise is vague. In order to answer it, one must interpret words or phrases to suit the needs of the conclusion.

After the discussion is over, you want the group to observe:

Who controlled or influenced the interpretations of those phrases?

Did group members listen to one another?

Did members of the group feel that what they had to say was listened to? Who did? Who didn't? (Ask individuals to respond.)

Were they able to make the contributions they wanted to make?

To what extent were the leadership patterns of this discussion similar to the patterns of other meetings you have experienced?

How was anger handled?

How were group deviants (those who wouldn't go along with the group norm) handled?

What might have been done to make the discussion a better one?

Did the time deadline affect the nature of the discussion? With more time, would they have been nicer to one another?

LEADERSHIP ISSUES IN GROUPS

Read through these statements individually, putting an "A" next to the ones you *agree* with and a "D" next to the ones with which you *disagree.*

Then, as a group, look over the statements and discuss those on which not all members of the group are in agreement. In any way you find suitable, try to reach consensus on as many of the statements as possible—either all members *agreeing* or all members *disagreeing* with the statement. You have half an hour. (*Key*: "A" = "agree." "D" = "disagree.")

1. A strong leader is able to achieve more than one who frequently consults his group before making a decision.

2. Since the figure of the rabbi/director/advisor/teacher, etc. always looms in the background, true self-government is an illusion.

3. The primary concern of all members of an organizational governing group/student government/board of directors, etc. should be to establish an atmosphere where all will feel free to express their opinions.

4. There are occasions when, in the midst of a project or planning a program, an individual should do what seems right, regardless of what the group has decided.

5. When the group has members who never seem to go along with the rest, the group must ignore their objections and proceed without them.

6. Almost any job that can be done by a committee can be done better by an individual, as long as a lot of physical work is not involved.

7. When an officer or leader is doing the best that can be done, one should not be openly critical or find fault with that person's conduct.

8. Democracy has but a limited role in an explicitly Jewish organization. Everyone should not have an equal say on things because everyone does not have an equal Jewish education or background.

9. Controversy is the best way to keep an organization together. There is nothing like a red-hot fight to keep members interested.

10. No group should expect all of its membership to be active. If a member never wants to do anything in the organization or come to events, that's a problem for that individual.

ROLE PLAY FOR AN ORGANIZATION OR CLASS

This may be done in as many groups of six to eight as have a staff member or trained assistant present. It is hard to make a role play work, at least in a large-group setting, without lots of warm-up and staff guidance. Instead of playing roles, the groups will often drift into just talking about the situations they are concerned with, and that is much less valuable. They will maintain roles only if the group is very experienced or the staff person keeps them on track, perhaps with that staff person also playing a role.

The role play described here is an institutional one. It could be anything else of interest as well. Allow 15–20 minutes for each person in a group.

ROLE PLAY

Think of a concrete situation in this group that you would like to be able to handle better that you think you can now.

It should be an interpersonal situation (e.g., a conversation you had or a meeting you will have to run) rather than an abstract one (e.g., how do you run a newspaper or what shall we do to deal with the unaffiliated?).

Describe briefly the setting and the characters, and add any other information needed to understand the situation.

Act out the situation with members of the group as the characters in your role play. You play yourself. When you are finished, let someone else who would deal with the matter differently take your part.

Let the group discuss the role plays.

Time matters so that everyone in the group will get a chance to act out situations and have them discussed.

EVALUATION

Be careful neither to neglect nor to overdo evaluation. Evaluation will help people clarify thoughts for themselves and also let you know what is happening. To start an oral evaluation discussion, consider questions like the following:

Do discussions need more time than you have been allowed?

Are things moving too slowly?

These are issues you can find out about in the evaluation discussions, as long as you don't overuse them. A couple of times a session is the maximum. The larger the total group, the less useful the general discussion will be. If there are more than thirty, its utility drops off considerably. It takes too much effort to get people quiet, and they will not all be as interested in one another's reports as the reporter or you may be.

Written evaluations can be informative but should not be used to the point where resistance develops. Here, too, once or twice is the maximum.

EVALUATION FORMS

There is an advantage to the particular forms included here over questionnaires that ask specific questions. In the latter the information is provided in predetermined areas. These tell you about things you might not have suspected, important matters of both a positive and negative nature.

The positive and negative reactions form would be suitable for larger events. This form is difficult to use if you want to quantify the results but is very helpful in providing a clear overview of what made an impact on the participants. The shorter form can be used for an overall evaluation of a weekend or for events as brief as a class or board meeting.

POSITIVE AND NEGATIVE REACTIONS

NAME _____

Write down fifteen significant *positive* things that you did or that happened—things that you liked and, that were important to you. If you wish to write more or fewer than fifteen items, feel free to do so. Where appropriate, be as specific as possible. (Don't just write "discussions," but name the topic or teacher as well; not just "services," but which service.)

1. _____

2. _____

3. _____

4. _____

5. _____

6. _____

7. _____

8. _____

9. _____

10. _____

11. _____

12. _____

13. _____

14. _____

15. _____

When you have listed as many items as you like, try to star(*) the five most important ones. Then, if you can, double star (**) the one that was most important to you.

Please turn page.

Now do the reverse. Write the things you felt most *negative* about and liked the least. Once again, try to star the five most significant items and double star the one you most disliked.

1. _____

2. _____

3. _____

4. _____

5. _____

6. _____

7. _____

8. _____

9. _____

10. _____

11. _____

12. _____

13. _____

14. _____

15. _____

If you have any other general comments to make, please write them here or attach a separate page. Return the questionnaire to a staff member.

A QUICK EVALUATION

In this group I like it when we...

In this group I wish we would...

FURTHER CAUTIONARY NOTES

In order to do these exercises you usually need a captive audience. People are not likely to attend an event that is advertised as one whose purpose is to enhance Jewish identity or to encourage reflection about the meaning of one's Jewishness. On the other hand, a group of people who show up for a more general purpose, such as a weekend retreat or a board meeting, may be quite delighted to participate in an activity that enhances the event they have come to.

Since they probably did not assent to such participation in advance, I believe that it is important, as a matter of both principle and technique, to make an honest contract with people before they become involved in any exercises. You can't always tell them precisely what they will be doing, but you can express the hope that they believe you when you explain that what they will be doing will be both enjoyable (hence the term "game") and significant. Make clear that you have no interest in forcing them to do anything they don't want to do. Encourage them to give things a try, but if they really feel imposed upon, let them feel that they do not have to continue and may sit quietly on the side. If a few drop out, they should be encouraged to join in again as soon as they feel comfortable in doing so. They should be sure not to bother those who are participating or make them feel self-conscious.

Some people are "cerebral" and really don't relate well to others when they have to talk about their feelings. Such people should be protected from having to do so.

At the height of the encounter movement people were extraordinarily sensitive to the possibility that someone might be manipulating them. Today, potential participants are less likely to be doctrinaire about the subject either pro or con. If there should be a large number of reluctants, encourage them to go off to the side or into another room and talk with one another about why they don't want to join in. Their position also deserves validation. When people know that they don't have to participate they generally feel a lot more relaxed about the situation and more able to take part. Although this issue was common in the past, it has been years since I have had enough reluctants to form a group of their own.

Once you have granted permission to drop out, do not constantly repeat it. It is now up to the participants. Proceed with the program on the assumption that all will join in unless they offer clues to the contrary or make explicit their desire not to do so.

If you find that many people refuse to participate, it may indicate that you were too hesitant in your instructions and the participants caught a tone of uncertainty. You are asking them to trust you. You must sound trustworthy. If you come across in a manner that suggests that you are hesitant about asking them to do this "weird" thing, but that it might be worth a few minutes of experimentation if a few would like to try, you are a dead duck. You will have no chance to get the thing off the ground, or, even worse, you will spend the rest of the meeting in a decision-making exercise with group members arguing about whether or not to get on with the games. If you come across firmly but non-punitively, then it is very unlikely that you will get more than one or two resisters.

Resistance is a little more complicated when it takes the form of someone coming to you in the middle of the exercise to tell you how they did something different (and probably better) in their psychology class, or to ask if you know cousin Charlie, who comes from the same place you do. Since it is very important that you be tuned in to the exercise that is taking place, you should gently suggest that you need to concentrate on the group activity that is in progress right now, and that there will be an opportunity to talk at one of the longer breaks you will be having.

A certain degree of "instant" intimacy is encouraged by these games. Do not let that intimacy get out of bounds. People have built their defenses carefully and for good reasons. They are entitled to keep them intact if they wish. Let them try to be as open as they comfortably can, but they should not discuss things about which they will have regrets the next day.

Do exercises with which *you* as a leader feel comfortable. Not all exercises are appropriate to all settings or for all people. If possible, find a way to pre-test them; for example, try them on a staff group. This will help you become sensitive to issues that future participants may also experience. You will discover aspects of the exercises you could not possibly know without having done them yourself.

You will probably not be able to be a participant in the exercises along with everyone else. Someone in the group needs to be aware of the time and notice when it is necessary to move on. That will be hard to do if you participate as a group member.

Anticipate your participant's moods before you choose a setting. If, for example, you were suddenly to spring exercises upon them in an ordinary coffeehouse setting, you would probably meet a lot of angry resistance. At such gatherings people generally want a reasonable degree of anonymity and the opportunity to drift in and out without making a serious commitment. On the other hand, a group gathered for an informal Shabbat afternoon discussion has time, is relaxed, and would probably be open to these kinds of experiences.

A WORRY LIST

When planning any of these activities, consider the following:

Have you planned your exercises in the light of your objectives?

How much total time is available?

Be sure to break down your individual exercises into estimated time slots. You need not stick firmly to these limits, but they will give you a much clearer notion of what you have to expand or cut short should you have to deviate from your original estimate.

It is essential that you work in a quiet and undisturbed environment. If you can't find such a place, don't bother to start.

Do you have an extra person who can even off the pairs if an odd number of people appears?

If your exercises require writing, do you have paper and pencils? Sharing pencils in such a setting never works out.

Do you have enough staff for the number of participants who might show up?

Will you need markers? Large sheets of paper? A blackboard and chalk?

Do you have a watch, preferably a stopwatch?

CONCLUSION AND BIBLIOGRAPHY

The exercises included here are meant to serve as illustrative examples. It is hoped that they will get you started and help you invent your own exercises in response to particular situations. There are a number of collections of exercises from which you may want to borrow. A few that may be of interest include:

Elkins, D.P. *Clarifying Jewish Values: Values Activities for Jewish Groups*. Rochester, NY: Growth Associates, 1977.

Elkins, D.P. *Jewish Consciousness Raising*. Rochester, NY: Growth Associates, 1977.

Lewis, H.R. & H.S. Streitfeld. *Growth Games*. New York: Bantam Books, 1970.

Malamud, D. & S. Machover. *Toward Self-Understanding: Group Techniques in Self-Confrontation*. Springfield, IL: Charles C. Thomas, 1965.

Pfeiffer, J.W. & J.E. Jones. *Handbooks of Structured Experiences for Human Relations Training. Volumes 1–11*. La Jolla, CA: University Associates, 1976.

Pfeiffer, J.W. & J.E. Jones. *Annual Handbooks for Group Facilitators*. La Jolla, CA: University Associates, 1972–1991.

Reisman, B. *Experiential Learning in Jewish Groups*: *Principles and Activities*. Waltham, MA: Brandeis University, 1975.

Reisman, B. *Routes to Jewish Identity: An Experimental Approach*. New York: Ktav, 1978.

Simon, S., L. Howe & H. Kirschenbaum. *Values Clarification: A Handbook of Practical Strategies*. Minneapolis: Winston Press, 1973.

The following groups and people are constantly developing new materials. You may want to be placed on their mailing lists. University Associates, NTL Learning Resources Corporation, and Growth Associates periodically publish catalogues. The materials of Growth Associates and Bernard Reisman are of specifically Jewish interest. The other two are not.

Growth Associates
Human Relations Consultants
P.O. Box 8429
Rochester, NY 14618

Bernard Reisman, Director
Hornstein Program in Jewish Communal Service
Brandeis University
Waltham, MA 02154

NTL Learning Resources Corporation
7594 Eads Avenue
La Jolla, CA 92037

University Associates
7594 Eads Avenue
La Jolla, CA 92037